TIGERS

Please visit our web site at: www.garethstevens.com
For a free color catalog describing Gareth Stevens Publishing's
list of high-quality books and multimedia programs, call
1-800-542-2595 (USA) or 1-800-387-3178 (Canada).
Gareth Stevens Publishing's fax: (414) 332-3567.

Library of Congress Cataloging-in-Publication Data

All about tigers.
   Tigers.
      p. cm. — (All about wild animals)
      Previously published in Great Britain as: All about tigers. 2002.
      ISBN 0-8368-4189-1 (lib. bdg.)
      1. Tigers—Juvenile literature. I. Title. II. Series.
   QL795.T5A445 2004
   599.756—dc22   2004041630

This edition first published in 2005 by
Gareth Stevens Publishing
A World Almanac Education Group Company
330 West Olive Street, Suite 100
Milwaukee, Wisconsin 53212 USA

This U.S. edition copyright © 2005 by Gareth Stevens, Inc. Original edition
copyright © 2002 by DeAgostini UK Limited. First published in 2002 as
My Animal Kingdom: All About Tigers by DeAgostini UK Ltd., Griffin House,
161 Hammersmith Road, London W6 8SD, England. Additional end matter
copyright © 2005 by Gareth Stevens, Inc.

Editorial and design: Tucker Slingsby Ltd., London
Gareth Stevens series editor: Catherine Gardner
Gareth Stevens art direction: Tammy West

Picture Credits
NHPA — Andy Rouse: front cover and title page, 15, 16, 18—19; John Shaw:
   6—7; Roger Tidman: 7, 11; Joe Blossom: 8; Yves Lanceau: 10; K. Ghani:
   11; E. A. Janes: 12; James Carmichael Jr.: 13; E. Hanumantha Rao: 15, 21,
   22; Gerard Lacz: 17, 19; Martin Harvey: 17, 22, 27; James Warwick: 20;
   Harry Teyn: 23; Daniel Heuchlin: 27; Dave Watts: 27; Martin Wendler: 29.
Oxford Scientific Films — Mike Hill: 9, 16; Alan and Sandy Carey: 10, 18, 24;
   Frank Schneidermever: 12—13; Michael Powles: 13; Bob Bennett: 14, 27;
   Belinda Wright: 19, 25, 29; Dieter and Mary Plage: 21; Vivek Sinha: 21;
   Krupaker Senani: 23; Stan Osolinski: 24; Norbert Rosing: 26; Mahipal
   Singh: 28; Stanley Breeden: 29.

ALL about WiLD ANiMaLS

TIGERS

Gareth Stevens Publishing
A WORLD ALMANAC EDUCATION GROUP COMPANY

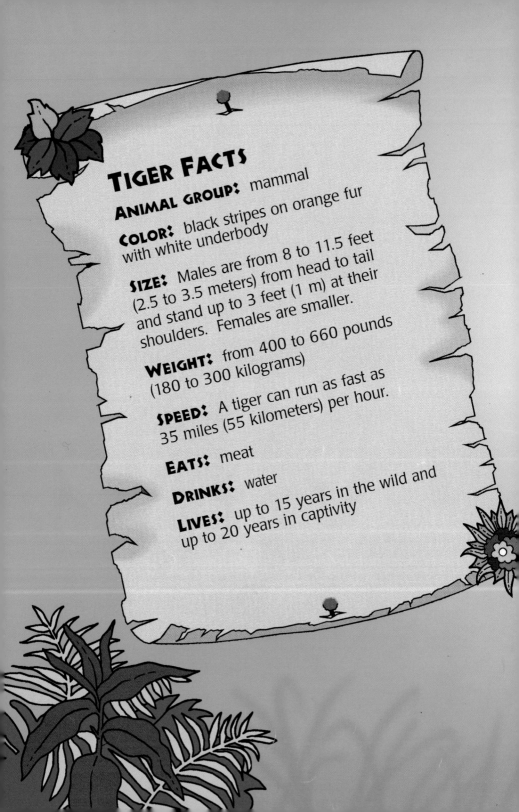

Tiger Facts

ANIMAL GROUP: mammal

COLOR: black stripes on orange fur with white underbody

SIZE: Males are from 8 to 11.5 feet (2.5 to 3.5 meters) from head to tail and stand up to 3 feet (1 m) at their shoulders. Females are smaller.

WEIGHT: from 400 to 660 pounds (180 to 300 kilograms)

SPEED: A tiger can run as fast as 35 miles (55 kilometers) per hour.

EATS: meat

DRINKS: water

LIVES: up to 15 years in the wild and up to 20 years in captivity

CONTENTS

Words that appear in the glossary
are printed in **boldface** type the
first time they occur in the text.

A Closer Look

Tigers are the biggest of the big cats, a group of related animals that includes leopards, jaguars, and lions. Five different types, or subspecies, of tigers live in the wild. The tigers from each subspecies are alike in many ways. They have boldly striped fur and powerful bodies. They spend most of the day resting. At dusk, they begin their hunt for **prey**. One key difference among the five types of tigers is their weight. A male Siberian tiger weighs up to 660 pounds (300 kilograms), while a male Sumatran tiger weighs only 265 pounds (120 kg).

I have big eyes and very good eyesight.

My strong jaws and sharp teeth help me catch animals to eat.

I have sharp claws for climbing trees and grabbing prey.

- The skin of a tiger has stripes, just like its fur!

- A tiger's stripes help it hide in the stripes of shade and light in the forest.

- The stripes on a tiger's fur are similar to the fingerprint of a person. Each tiger's fur coat has a different stripy pattern.

My striped fur coat helps me blend in among the shadows of the trees and long grass.

I have a strong body and legs, so I can run fast and catch animals heavier than I am.

When I run or climb, my long tail keeps me from losing my balance.

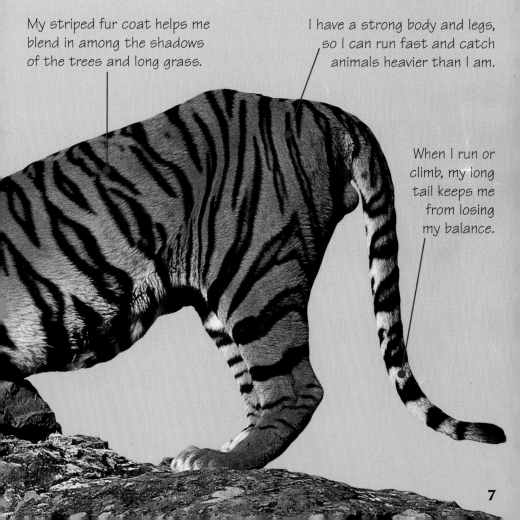

A tiger may look like a gentle cat, but it's not. It is one of the fiercest **predators** in the world. It can kill animals twice its size with its powerful jaws. Tigers have big eyes and ears and sharp senses. They can see six times more clearly than a human in the dark, and they can hear five times better than humans. They use their sense of smell to locate prey and to detect the **scents** left by other tigers.

NIGHT EYES

At night, a tiger's eyes seem to glow brightly. The glow is caused by a surface at the back of each eye that acts like a mirror. When light enters a tiger's eye, it hits this surface and bounces back into the eye. The light that bounces back helps the tiger see clearly in dim light. No wonder tigers are such great hunters in the dark!

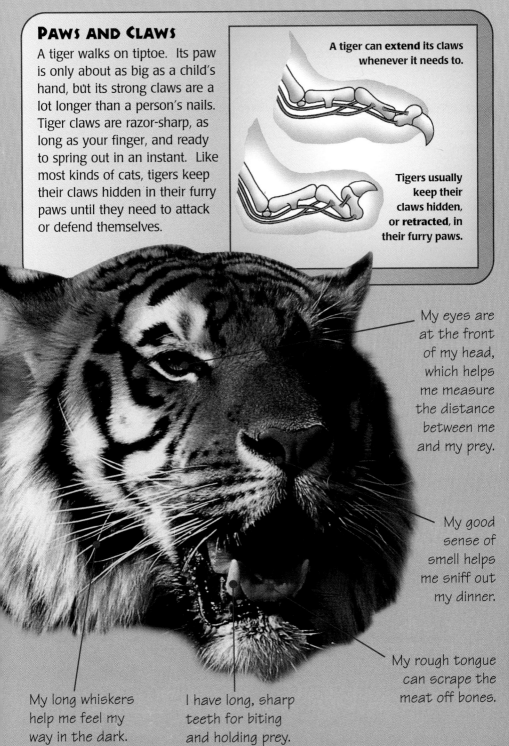

PAWS AND CLAWS

A tiger walks on tiptoe. Its paw is only about as big as a child's hand, but its strong claws are a lot longer than a person's nails. Tiger claws are razor-sharp, as long as your finger, and ready to spring out in an instant. Like most kinds of cats, tigers keep their claws hidden in their furry paws until they need to attack or defend themselves.

A tiger can **extend its claws** whenever it needs to.

Tigers usually keep their claws hidden, or **retracted**, in their furry paws.

My eyes are at the front of my head, which helps me measure the distance between me and my prey.

My good sense of smell helps me sniff out my dinner.

My rough tongue can scrape the meat off bones.

My long whiskers help me feel my way in the dark.

I have long, sharp teeth for biting and holding prey.

9

HOME, SWEET HOME

All wild tigers live in Asia. Tigers live in forests and avoid areas of open grassland. Some types of tigers live in the hot, steamy jungles of India, while other types survive in the icy-cold forests of Siberia. All types of tigers need a lot of space in which to live and hunt. In many parts of Asia, people are destroying the tiger's **habitat** by cutting down forests and building more farms and cities.

DID YOU KNOW?

Most types of tigers live in warm places, but Siberian tigers have a cold home. Siberian tigers are the largest of all the big cats. They have thick fur coats that keep them warm, even in bitterly cold weather. During the winter months, their fur becomes lighter in color, helping to **camouflage** them in the snow. Only about two hundred Siberian tigers still live in the wild.

HIDING AWAY

A tiger has at least one den in its **home range** and usually has several dens. A den is a sheltered area where a tiger can rest and stay cool during the hottest part of the day. A tiger also drags food back to the den to eat. Sometimes, a tiger buries its leftover food outside in the leaves to keep it safe from other animals that might steal its meal.

WHERE IN THE WORLD?

Thousands of tigers once roamed the forests of the Middle East and Southeast Asia. Over the years, many tigers were hunted and killed. Today, tigers remain in only a few parts of Asia. One hundred years ago, more than 100,000 tigers lived in the wild. Now, only 5,000 to 7,000 wild tigers are still alive. Some countries have tiger **sanctuaries**, where hunting is not allowed.

Neighbors

Bengal tigers live in the hot forests of India. Colorful birds and butterflies fly among the tree branches there. Spiders and snakes hide in the leaves. Porcupines, tortoises, and lizards crawl across the forest floor. Monkeys and deer make tasty meals for a tiger, but elephants, rhinoceroses, and **water buffaloes** are much too dangerous for a tiger to hunt.

Fabulous Fan

The Indian peacock's shimmering tail has more than two hundred glittering patterns that look like eyes. He struts about, spreading out his tail to attract females, called peahens. If a peahen or a peacock sees a **prowling** tiger, it lets out a frightful screech to warn the others because tigers snack on peafowl.

Grazing Gaur

Small herds of gaur live in hilly forests, grazing on low-growing plants. The huge male, with its massive head and thick horns, is a fearsome enemy, but an old, sick, or baby gaur is an easy catch for a tiger.

MONKEY BUSINESS

Langur monkeys are a noisy bunch. They scream to each other as they swing from tree to tree, searching for food. The Hanuman langur, a type of langur monkey named for the Hindu monkey god, is sacred to people who practice the Hindu faith. Lucky Hanuman monkeys often find tasty treats left behind for them in Hindu temples.

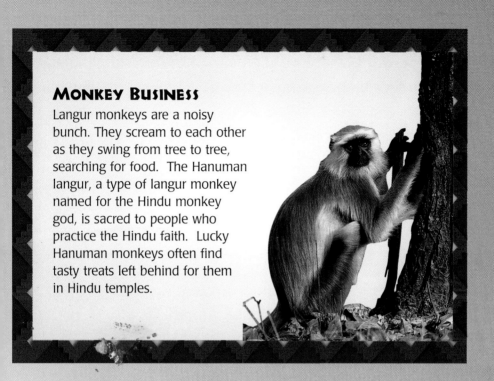

STRIPED HUNTER

The Indian ornamental spider is huge and hairy. This spider can grow to be bigger than a child's hand! Like a tiger, the striped Indian ornamental spider is a predator. The spider hides in tree hollows and underneath loose bark, waiting to **pounce** on any passing prey.

THE FAMILY

Tigers do not live in family groups. They spend almost all of their lives alone. A male tiger has a home range where he hunts and sleeps. He does not allow any other male tigers to enter his home range. To keep other tigers off of his land, a male marks the trees in his home range with claw scratches and scents. A male tiger's range can overlap with areas used by several females. Adult tigers do not meet often, except to **mate**.

A female tiger, called a tigress, raises a **litter** of two to four cubs every two or three years. The father of the cubs does not live with the family or help care for them in any way. The mother must feed, clean, teach, and guard her cubs on her own for

over two years. When she leaves her cubs to hunt, she hides them in the **undergrowth** or in her den.

BABY BLUES

Tiger cubs are born with blue eyes and pale stripes. As the cubs get older, their stripes darken and their eyes turn a golden yellow.

MOM'S MILK

A newborn tiger cub drinks its mother's milk. After a few months, she brings meaty treats to build up the cub's strength.

DID YOU KNOW?

- Tigers purr, but their purrs are different from the purrs of pet cats. Pet cats purr as they breathe in and as they breathe out. Tigers can only purr as they breathe out.

- Tigers look as if they have eyes on the backs of their ears! Two spots that look like eyes are really patches of black and white fur that help a cub spot its mother as she prowls in the forest.

BABY FILE

BIRTH

Newborn tiger cubs are tiny. They cannot see for the first ten days of their lives, so they depend totally on their mothers. A cub spends most of the day feeding on its mother's milk and being **groomed** with her rough tongue.

THREE TO SIX MONTHS

By the age of three months, cubs eat meat their mothers bring them. They learn to hunt by play-fighting with each other and pouncing on their mothers' tails.

ONE TO THREE YEARS

When cubs are about one year old, they hunt with the tigresses. They watch and copy their mothers. At first, they do not catch much, but in a year or two, they hunt alone.

LIFE ON THE MOVE

A tiger's body is built to move in many different ways. The tiger has a tough, bendy backbone, so it can leap and pounce. Its long, strong legs help this big cat run and jump. Its long tail maintains the tiger's balance as it runs and turns while chasing its prey. Tigers are able to climb and swim, too.

WATER BABIES

Unlike most other cats, tigers like water. They can swim well, but they try not to let their faces get wet! To cool off on a hot day, tigers like to swim in a river or lie at the edge of a swampy pond. They also drink lots of water, especially after they eat a big meal.

COOL CLIMBER

Like pet cats, tigers are able to climb trees. They use their strong legs and sharp claws to help them scamper up into the tree branches.

LONG LEAPS

Tigers can jump over walls that are 6 feet (2 meters) tall while carrying their prey. They can cover over 32 feet (10 m) — the length of two small cars — in one leap.

FAVORITE FOODS

Most of the time, tigers eat the large hooved **mammals** that live in their habitat. One favorite food is deer, which they hunt at night. To catch its prey, a tiger creeps up on an animal until it is about 52 feet (16 m) away. Then it bounds forward and pounces. Tigers are skilled hunters, but they do not always get their prey. They catch about one out of every ten to twenty animals they hunt.

DEER DIET
Herds of spotted deer, called chital, keep a sharp lookout for tigers as they graze in the shady forests. A tiger's favorite dinner is deer or cattle.

Easy Meal

Hunting is difficult, especially for older tigers. Sometimes they try a trick to catch an easy meal. A tiger hides under a tree where some monkeys are resting. Suddenly, the tiger roars loudly, scaring the young monkeys. If the tiger is lucky, a monkey becomes so scared that it falls out of the tree into the tiger's jaws!

DID YOU KNOW?

- A tiger can eat up to 65 pounds (30 kg) of meat a night.

- A tiger's canine teeth are nearly 3 inches (7.6 centimeters) long.

- Tigers can snap bones in one bite.

- A tiger can kill an animal that is more than twice its own weight.

Prickly Mouthful

Tigers usually eat deer and other big animals, but hungry tigers eat almost anything. They gobble up monkeys, fish, lizards, and prickly porcupines! If they cannot make a kill, they eat old or rotting meat.

21

Danger!

Adult tigers are too big and fierce to have any enemies — except humans. Tiger cubs are not so lucky. Unlike lion cubs, young tigers have no one to look after them while their mothers hunt. Before a mother tiger starts hunting, she hides her cubs in the undergrowth. Once in a while, a predator attacks a cub in its hiding place. A tiger cub makes a meal for a python, leopard, or wild dog.

Leaping Leopards

Leopards are always looking for their next meal. They hide in a tree or lurk in the grass waiting for a prey animal to wander by. A leopard kills its prey by biting its throat or the back of its neck. Then it carries the animal away to eat later in a safe place.

Silent Hunter

The slender Indian python can eat large prey. This python grows up to 20 feet (6 m) long, and it can swallow a tiger cub in one gulp!

DEADLY DOGS

Asian wild dogs are called dholes. Family groups of dholes join to hunt in a pack. A pack of dholes can bring down prey as large as a buffalo. A hungry dhole can eat 10 pounds (4.5 kg) of meat in less than one hour! A lone tiger cub is easy prey for these deadly dogs.

BEWARE THE BEAR

The Siberian tiger shares its home with a fierce neighbor — the brown bear. A brown bear can grow as big as three tigers and weigh more than seven grown humans! A brown bear is able to attack and kill a grown tiger, especially if the bear has cubs to protect.

A Tiger's Day

6:00 AM
My cubs woke up at sunrise. They were hungry for a drink of my milk. I spent the night hunting, but it is hard to sleep with growing cubs.

7:00 AM
The cubs finished feeding. I dozed, flicking my tail so the cubs would try to leap on it. That's good practice for young hunters.

9:00 AM
Birds squawked and monkeys howled as our neighbors began to wake. The cubs napped peacefully through the forest noise. Our den was cozy, so I snoozed, too.

11:00 AM
The cubs woke and started to play-fight, rolling around in a tangle of claws, paws, and fur. Ouch! That was my tail!

12 NOON
The weather was very hot. I took my cubs to the pond for a long drink and a cool swim.

4:00 PM
My cubs were hungry, so we walked to a nearby den where I could feed them. I had part of a deer hidden there.

6:00 PM

The cubs were full and happy. I washed them, and they purred loudly. They quickly fell asleep. I napped, too. It would soon be time to go hunting.

8:00 PM

My cubs had the last, sleepy drink of milk for the night. I lifted them gently by the skin at the back of their necks and carried them into the undergrowth to hide.

10:00 PM

Quietly, I crept to the river and hid in the long grass. I waited, watching a herd of chital deer drink. I pounced out on one female deer, but it escaped.

1:00 AM

After a long wait, I managed to surprise a big male deer. He ran into the water, and I caught him easily. Then I had to drag dinner back to the cubs. What hard work!

2:00 AM

We ate and drank our fill, then I buried the remains of the deer in the leaves. A prowling leopard came near. I let out a huge roar, and he soon went away.

4:00 AM

The cubs are asleep. After that big meal, I will not need to hunt for the next few days. I can relax and sleep for a few hours. My cubs will be up soon.

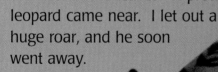

RELATIVES

Tigers have many relatives. There are thirty-six species, or kinds, of cats living all around the world. Wild cats live on every continent except Australia and Antarctica. Over half of the cat species live in Asia with tigers. The cat family is split into two main groups — big cats, such as tigers, and small cats, such as pumas. Big cats are known for their mighty roars, but small cats cannot roar.

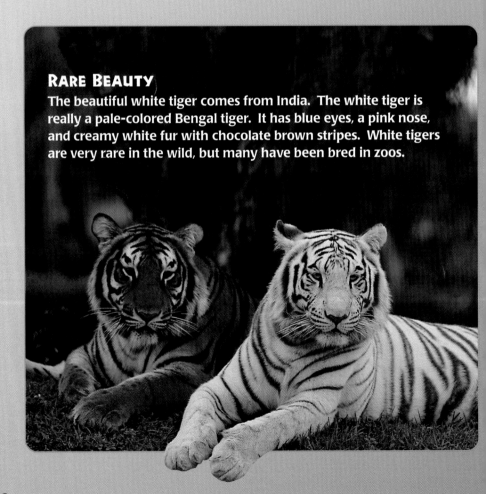

RARE BEAUTY
The beautiful white tiger comes from India. The white tiger is really a pale-colored Bengal tiger. It has blue eyes, a pink nose, and creamy white fur with chocolate brown stripes. White tigers are very rare in the wild, but many have been bred in zoos.

• The ancient saber-toothed tigers were not really tigers. They belonged to a branch of the cat family that died out about eight thousand years ago. They were fierce predators that used their long, pointed teeth to kill their prey.

• An animal called the Tasmanian tiger became extinct in the 1930s. It may have been a striped hunter, but it was not a big cat. It was a marsupial, like a kangaroo.

TUFTY

Twenty-eight kinds of small cats live in the world. The caracal is one kind of small cat. It lives in dry, semidesert areas of Africa and Asia. The caracal is hard to see on dry grassland. Its yellow fur blends in with the sandy soil, and its long ear tufts look like the tips of grasses.

WILD OR TAME?

The wild fishing cat (*top*) looks like a pet cat but has very special feet. The fishing cat lives in the swamps of Asia and eats fish. To help it speed through the water with its prey, the fishing cat has webbed feet. It has claws like fishhooks to hang onto its slippery prey.

Humans and Tigers

Tigers have fascinated and frightened people throughout history. People have used tigers in art and in books. At one time, some people kept tigers as pets. Other people have viewed tigers as pests. They have hunted tigers for sport and for their fur and killed tigers that tried to eat farm animals. Today, very few tigers remain in the wild. Most tigers live in parks where hunting is not allowed.

Year of the Tiger

Chinese New Year is a really fun festival. People dress up and march in street parades with bright paper models of dragons, rats, pigs, lions, and tigers. The festival lasts for a month! Each year is named after one of twelve different animals. People born in the Year of the Tiger are thought to be brave and fearless, just like a tiger!

SAVE THE TIGER

Many groups of people are now trying to protect wild tigers. For many years, the World Wildlife Fund (WWF) has tried to save wild tigers. In 1972, it started Operation Tiger, and over the next twenty years, the numbers of tigers increased. Today, tigers are still under threat from humans, so in 1998, the WWF started another worldwide effort to save tigers.

DID YOU KNOW?

Many tigers are in danger. Hunters want their fur, and farmers want to cut down their forest homes to make farmland. During the past seventy years, the Caspian, Balinese, and Javan types of tigers have all died out in the wild.

Glossary

CAMOUFLAGE
To have a color, pattern, or appearance that helps an animal blend in with its surroundings.

EXTEND
To lengthen or stretch out.

GROOMED
Taken care of, especially hair or fur, by removing dirt and making it neat and attractive.

HABITAT
The natural setting in which a plant or animal lives.

HOME RANGE
An animal's territory, the area of land it claims for hunting and defends against other animals of its kind.

LITTER
A group of young born to one mother at the same time.

MAMMALS
Warm-blooded animals that have backbones, that have hair or fur on their skin, and that feed their young with milk from the mothers' bodies.

MATE
To come together for the purpose of producing young.

POUNCE
To jump on top of something suddenly and unexpectedly.

PREDATORS
Animals that hunt other animals for food.

PREY
Animals that another animal hunts and kills for food.

PROWLING
Moving silently and secretly while looking for something.

RETRACTED
Pulled back or inside a covering.

SANCTUARIES
Areas of land set aside as places where wild animals and plants can live in their natural surroundings without being disturbed or harmed by humans.

SCENTS
Odors produced and left by animals on any surface they have walked on or touched.

UNDERGROWTH
Thick shrubs and grasses covering the ground.

WATER BUFFALOES
Buffaloes of a type found mostly in swampy or frequently flooded areas, especially in southern Asia. They have thick, wide horns that curve inward and backward.

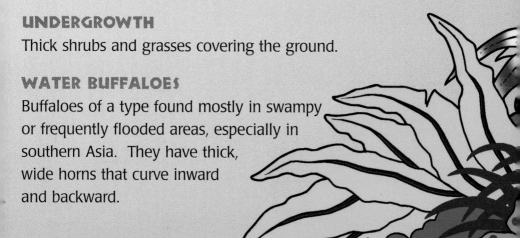

INDEX